D1233419

Clay Matthews

By Jeff Savage

AMAZING ATHLETES

Lerner Publications Company • Minneapolis

For Jason Wallom—whose fierce determination matches that of Clay Matthews

Lerner Publications Company
A division of Lerner Publishing Group, Inc.
241 First Avenue North
Minneapolis, MN 55401 U.S.A.

Website address: www.lernerbooks.com

Library of Congress Cataloging-in-Publication Data

Savage, Jeff, 1961–
    Clay Matthews / by Jeff Savage.
       p.   cm. — (Amazing athletes)
    Includes index.
    ISBN 978–1–4677–0307–9 (lib. bdg. : alk. paper)
    1. Matthews, Clay, 1986–—Juvenile literature. 2. Football players—United States—Biography—Juvenile literature I. Title.
    GV939.M2964S28 2013
    796.332092—dc23 [B]   2012010084

Manufactured in the United States of America
1 – BP – 7/15/12

TABLE OF CONTENTS

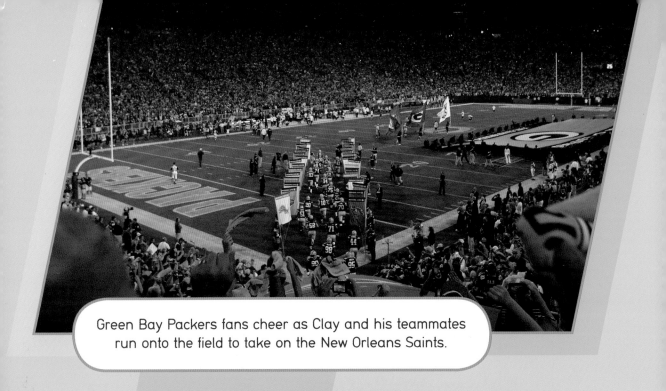

Green Bay Packers fans cheer as Clay and his teammates run onto the field to take on the New Orleans Saints.

THE PREDATOR

Clay Matthews was ready. The football was snapped. New Orleans Saints **quarterback** Drew Brees dropped back to pass. Clay rushed toward him. An **offensive lineman** tried to **block** Clay. Clay broke free. He slammed into Brees. The pass fell to the turf. Clay celebrated his big play. He squatted wide and spread out his arms. He leaned back and howled. The pose is called the Predator, after the monster from the *Predator* movies.

Clay is the rock-solid **linebacker** for the Green Bay Packers. He stands 6 feet 3 inches and weighs 255 pounds. His muscles bulge under his shoulder pads. His long blond hair flies wildly as he tackles ball carriers. Clay is fast, powerful, and nearly impossible to stop.

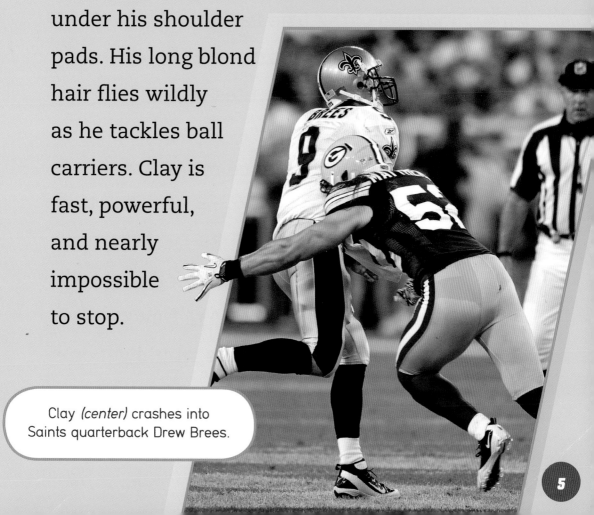

Clay *(center)* crashes into Saints quarterback Drew Brees.

Clay and his teammates were playing the Saints in their first game of the 2011–2012 National Football League (NFL) season. The Packers were the defending Super Bowl champions. The Saints had a high-powered offense. As expected, the teams battled hard throughout the game. The Packers held a 42–27 lead late in the fourth quarter. But Brees threw a touchdown with two minutes to go. The score was now 42–34.

The Saints got the ball once more. Brees marched his team to the Packers' nine-yard line. Three seconds remained. Brees threw a pass into the **end zone**. The ball fell to the ground. But Packers' **defender** A. J. Hawk committed a penalty. The Saints would get one last chance to tie the game.

The football was placed at the one-yard line.

The Saints needed one yard for a touchdown. Saints **running back** Mark Ingram took the ball. Clay blasted through the blocks. He grabbed Ingram. More Packers swarmed in. Clay and his teammates stopped Ingram short of the end zone. The Packers won the game!

"I think it's fantastic to get the stop that we needed and get off the field with the victory," said Clay.

Clay *(right)* grabs Mark Ingram before Ingram can score a touchdown.

Clay grew up near Los Angeles, California.

FAST AND FASTER

William Clay Matthews III was born May 14, 1986, in Northridge, California. He grew up in Agoura Hills, near Los Angeles. Clay is one of five children born to Leslie and Clay Matthews Jr. His older sister is Jennifer. His older brothers are Kyle and Brian. His younger brother is Casey.

Clay grew up in a football family. His father, Clay Jr., played linebacker for the Cleveland Browns and the Atlanta Falcons. His uncle, Bruce Matthews, reached the NFL **Hall of Fame** after playing offensive lineman for the Houston Oilers and the Tennessee Titans. His grandfather, Clay, was an offensive lineman for the San Francisco 49ers. His brother, Casey, plays linebacker for the Philadelphia Eagles.

Clay's father *(right)* played in the NFL for 19 years. He is shown here in his Cleveland Browns uniform.

Clay wears small-sized shoulder pads. "I like everything tight and small," he says. "If you leave stuff out there for those offensive linemen to grab, they're going to hold you all day."

Clay was an active boy. "He plays now like he was as a kid," says his mother. "He has two speeds—fast and faster." Clay was seven years old when he suffered a serious head injury crashing on his skateboard. It did not slow him down. He enjoyed jumping from the roof of his house onto a trampoline and into the backyard swimming pool. At the age of nine, he joined his first tackle football team. He loved bashing into opponents. "He never gave me a problem," his mother says, "except worrying about his safety."

Clay was a bright student. At Agoura High School, he earned excellent grades. But he struggled on the football field. Clay wanted

Clay worked hard in high school to become bigger and stronger.

to play linebacker. His father coached the defense. He thought Clay was too skinny to play such a tough position. As a junior, Clay mostly sat on the bench. "He wasn't ready," Clay's father said. "He wasn't very big and he wasn't very strong." Clay finally became a starter as a senior. He played well, but he hadn't played enough for colleges to notice him.

Clay thought he could be a star player at the University of Southern California (USC). Clay's father and uncle had played for the school. The USC Trojans have long been a football powerhouse. Clay decided he would try to make the team as a **walk-on**.

"When he told us that is what he wanted, we were surprised but supportive," said his mother. Agoura High School's head coach Charlie Wegher had his doubts. "I told him to go for it," the coach said. "But honestly, I didn't think he'd get a chance to play much." The only person who truly believed he could do it was Clay himself.

The USC Trojans play their home games at Los Angeles Memorial Coliseum.

SKINNY WALK-ON

Clay arrived at USC in 2004 with confidence. Coach Pete Carroll gave him a uniform. The Trojans had stars like quarterback Matt Leinart and running back Reggie Bush. Clay imagined himself as another star. "I thought I could come in here, day one, and be the guy," said Clay. "Maybe I was crazy. But obviously that's better than saying you can't."

Clay *(center)* poses for a photo with his parents.

Clay made the team. But he sat on the bench during games. He never played. "I didn't have a lot of friends," he said. "I was the skinny walk-on." USC crushed opponents on their way to winning the 2004 national title.

In the last few minutes of games, Coach Carroll would ask, "Clay, do you want to go in?" Clay said no every time. By not playing in 2004, he would still be thought of as a freshman for the 2005 season. College athletes are only allowed to play for four years. By not playing during his first year, Clay would be allowed to play four more years at USC.

As a **redshirt** freshman in 2005, Clay sat again. But he didn't give up. "My dad was a late bloomer too," Clay said. "I just kept working as hard as I could, getting stronger and faster." Clay lifted weights. He ran sprints. The coaches noticed. "He had a certain drive about him," said linebackers coach Ken Norton Jr.

Former USC linebackers coach Ken Norton Jr. *(right)* played for the Dallas Cowboys and San Francsico 49ers in the NFL.

Clay was a starter on his high school team only as a senior. He was a starter at USC only as a senior.

As a sophomore in 2006, Clay was rewarded with an **athletic scholarship**. He still wasn't part of the starting defense. But he did play on **special teams**. He made great plays and was named USC's Co-Special Teams Player of the Year. As a junior in 2007, he won the award again. But Clay wasn't satisfied. He worked harder.

In 2008, Clay was a beast on the field. He had gained 60 pounds since arriving at USC. A lot of the weight was muscle. He stood 6 feet 3 inches and weighed 240 pounds. "He gives a lot of hope to a lot of guys because he wasn't big enough and he wasn't fast enough, but he is now," said Coach Carroll. "Now he's perfect."

A special position was created for Clay. It was called Elephant. Clay got to line up where he wanted. He could stand anywhere on the field. Clay made big plays. He helped USC become the nation's top-ranked defense. He was ready to move to the next level.

Clay *(center)* made big plays all over the field in 2008.

Green Bay Packers linebackers coach Kevin Greene *(above)* liked what he saw in Clay. Greene also had a great NFL career as a star linebacker.

HARD WORK PAYS OFF

Clay had built himself into a football star. He posed for the cover of *Sports Illustrated* magazine. But he had more than fame on his mind early in 2009.

The 2009 NFL **draft** was held on April 25. **Scouts** wondered if Clay could be a playmaker in football's top league. The Green Bay Packers had no doubt. "I saw heart. I saw a motor. I saw a passion," said Packers linebackers coach Kevin Greene. "I saw a kid who, with a little polish here or there, could be a stone-cold diamond." The Packers selected Clay.

In 2009, the Green Bay Packers did not have a first-round draft pick. So they traded with the New England Patriots to get the 26th overall pick. They used it to select Clay.

Clay joined a team on the rise. The offense was improving with Aaron Rodgers at quarterback. It was Clay's job to help the defense. It didn't take him long to make an impact.

The Packers played the Minnesota Vikings on *Monday Night Football* on October 5, 2009. With millions of people watching, Vikings running back Adrian Peterson ran left with the football. Clay ripped the ball from Peterson's arms. Clay sprinted down the field 42 yards and into the end zone. He celebrated his first NFL touchdown by throwing the football into the stands.

Two weeks later against the Detroit Lions, Clay **sacked** quarterback Daunte Culpepper twice.

Clay raises his arm in celebration as he goes into the end zone for his first NFL touchdown.

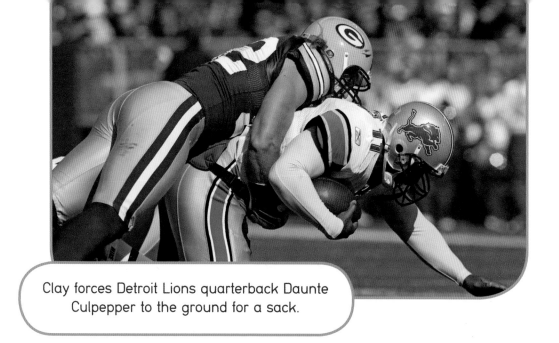

Clay forces Detroit Lions quarterback Daunte Culpepper to the ground for a sack.

Clay was named NFL **Rookie** of the Week. Against the Dallas Cowboys, he sacked Tony Romo and recovered two **fumbles** to win the rookie award again.

Other teams began using two blockers to try to stop Clay. But they couldn't slow him down. Against the Pittsburgh Steelers, he sacked Ben Roethlisberger twice. By doing so, Clay set a Packers' season record for most sacks by a rookie. Green Bay reached the **playoffs** but lost in the first round.

Clay was suddenly more famous than ever. Fans around the country knew about the linebacker with the flowing blond hair. He even appeared in a TV ad where he came alive from a poster and made the Predator pose. Clay liked the attention. He enjoyed winning even more.

Fans were getting used to seeing Clay celebrate big plays on the field.

Clay takes down Philadelphia Eagles quarterback Michael Vick during the first game of the 2010–2011 season.

SUPER BOWL

The Packers changed their defense for the 2010–2011 season. Clay was allowed to line up where he wanted, as he did at USC.

In the season opener at Philadelphia, Clay sacked the quarterback three times. One week later, against the Buffalo Bills, Clay got three more sacks. Against the Dallas Cowboys in week nine, Clay **intercepted** his first pass. He returned it 62 yards for a touchdown.

The Packers won their last two regular season games to sneak into the playoffs. They had to win three games on the road to reach the Super Bowl. Clay and his teammates beat the Philadelphia

Clay *(left)* returns his first-ever interception for a touchdown.

Eagles, the Atlanta Falcons, and the Chicago Bears. The Packers were headed to the Super Bowl! They would face the Pittsburgh Steelers.

The Packers led, 21–17, in the fourth quarter. The Steelers had the ball 33 yards from the end zone. That's when Clay made the defensive play of the game. Pittsburgh's running back Rashard Mendenhall took the ball up the middle. Clay slammed into him. The hit knocked the ball loose. Packers defender Desmond Bishop recovered the fumble.

Clay *(second from left)* tackles Rashard Mendenhall. Clay's tackle caused Mendenhall to fumble the ball.

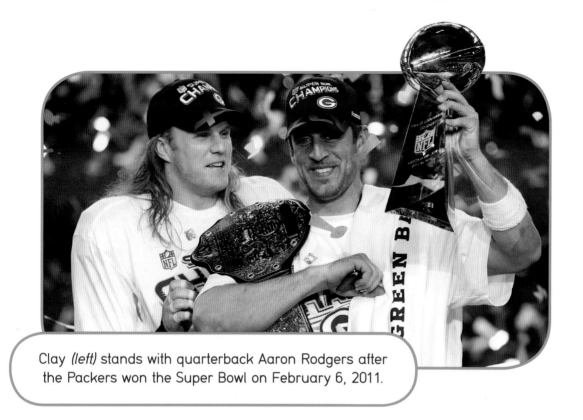

Clay *(left)* stands with quarterback Aaron Rodgers after the Packers won the Super Bowl on February 6, 2011.

The Packers held on to win the game, 31–25. "You play to be world champions," Clay said. "And that's what we are today."

How do you top winning a Super Bowl title? In 2011, the Packers tried. They roared through most of the season without losing a game. Along the way, they lost several defenders to injury. Clay kept the defense focused. Green Bay had a 13–0 record with three games to go.

But their winning streak ended in Kansas City against the Chiefs. They finished with a 15–1 record. The Packers lost to the New York Giants in the playoffs, 37–20.

Clay made 17 sacks in his first 20 games as a pro. It was the most ever by an NFL player at the start of his career.

Clay tackles running back Ahmad Bradshaw during Green Bay's 37–20 playoff loss to the New York Giants.

Clay is proud to wear a Super Bowl ring. But he doesn't brag about it "I try to stay humble. I'm just going to try to get back to the Super Bowl the old-fashioned way—hard work." Clay knows that hard work is the key to success. "It's not where you start," he says. "It's where you finish."

Clay signs autographs for fans before the start of the 2011–2012 season.

Selected Career Highlights

2011 Voted to the Pro Bowl for the third time
Had career-high three interceptions and three
   forced fumbles

2010 Helped Packers to victory in Super Bowl XLV
Named *Sporting News* NFL Defensive Player of
   the Year
Named National Football Conference (NFC)
   Defensive Player of the Year
Named Butkus Award winner as NFL's top
   linebacker
Named First Team All-Pro
Voted to the Pro Bowl for the second time
Ranked fourth in the NFL in sacks with 13.5

2009 Voted to his first Pro Bowl, becoming first Packers rookie in over 30
years so honored
Named NFC Defensive Rookie of the Year
Named NFL Rookie of the Week twice
Named NFC Player of the Week
Recorded 10 sacks

2008 Named to Pac-10 All-Academic Team
Totaled 57 tackles, including nine for losses
Recorded 4.5 sacks
Forced two fumbles
Blocked one field goal

2007 Named USC's Co-Special Teams Player of the Year
Totaled 17 tackles, including three for losses
Forced two fumbles
Blocked two field goals

2006 Named USC's Co-Special Teams Player of the Year
Received athletic scholarship

2004 Made the USC football team as a walk-on

Glossary

athletic scholarship: money given to a college player to help pay the cost of his or her education

block: in football, to get in the way of a player on the other team to slow or stop him

defender: a player whose job it is to stop the other team from scoring

draft: a yearly event in which professional teams take turns choosing new players from a selected group

end zone: the area beyond the goal line at each end of a football field. A team scores a touchdown when it reaches the other team's end zone.

fumbles: when a football player loses his hold on the ball

Hall of Fame: In pro football, the organization that showcases the best football players from previous years. Journalists vote for those who end up in the Hall of Fame.

intercepted: when a pass is caught by a person on the other team. An interception results in the opposing team getting possession of the ball.

linebacker: a defender who guards against both the run and the pass

offensive lineman: a football player who blocks for the quarterback and the ball carriers

playoffs: a series of games held every year to decide a champion

quarterback: a football player whose main job is to throw passes

redshirt: a second-year freshman

rookie: a first-year player

running back: a football player whose main job is to run with the ball

sacked: the tackling of a quarterback with the football for a loss of yards

scouts: football experts who watch players closely to judge their ability

special teams: teams other than offense and defense, such as kickoff and punt teams

walk-on: a player who tries out for a college team and is allowed to join but is not given a scholarship

Further Reading & Websites

Kennedy, Mike, and Mark Stewart. *Touchdown: The Power and Precision of Football's Perfect Play*. Minneapolis: Millbrook Press, 2010.

Savage, Jeff. *Aaron Rodgers*. Minneapolis: Lerner Publications Company, 2012.

Savage, Jeff. *Drew Brees*. Minneapolis: Lerner Publications Company, 2011.

Clay Matthews: The Official Site
http://www.claymatthews52.com
Clay's official site features a biography, photos, an online store, and access to Clay's Facebook page and Twitter account.

Green Bay Packers: The Official Site
http://www.packers.com/
The official website of the Green Bay Packers includes the team schedule and game results, late-breaking news, the team history, biographies of players like Clay Matthews, and much more.

The Official Site of the National Football League
http://www.nfl.com
The NFL's official website provides fans with the latest scores, schedules, and standings, biographies and statistics of players, as well as the league's official online store.

Sports Illustrated Kids
http://www.sikids.com
The *Sports Illustrated Kids* website covers all sports, including the NFL.

Index

Photo Acknowledgments

The images in this book are used with the permission of: © Jonathan Daniel/Getty Images, pp. 4, 22, 27; AP Photo/Paul Spinelli, pp. 5, 7; © Andy Z./Shutterstock.com, p. 8; © George Gojkovich/Getty Images, p. 9; Seth Poppel Yearbook Library, p. 11; © Lisa Blumenfeld/Getty Images, p. 13; © Jeff Golden/Getty Images, p. 14; © Stephen Dunn/Getty Images, p. 15; Jeff Lewis/Icon SMI/Newscom, p. 17; AP Photo/David Stluka, p. 18; Mark Hoffman/MCT/Newscom, p. 20; AP Photo/Jeffrey Phelps, p. 21; © Hunter Martin/Getty Images, p. 23; Benny Sieu/MCT/Newscom, p. 24; Jeff Haynes/REUTERS/Newscom, p. 25; © Jamie Squire/Getty Images, p. 26; AP Photo/Morry Gash, p. 28; © Joe Robbins/Getty Images, p. 29.

Front cover: AP Photo/Mike McCarn.

Main body text set in Caecilia LT Std 55 Roman 16/28.
Typeface provided by Adobe Systems.